The Tao
of the
Huainan Masters

The Tao
of the
Huainan Masters

Rosemary brant

Astrolog Publishing House

Cover Design: Na'ama Yaffe

Production Manager: Dan Gold

P.O. Box 1123, Hod Hasharon 45111, Israel
Tel: 972-9-7412044
Fax: 972-97442714

© Astrolog Publishing House Ltd. 2005

ISBN 965-494-187-2

Published by Astrolog Publishing House 2005

The The Tao of the Huainan Masters is a collection of phrases and extracts from Huainanzi, also known as The Masters of Huainan. This classic is considered one of the most important Taoist texts.

According to tradition, a group of teachers gathered in king Huainan's court and began studying and teaching Taoist philosophy, based on and extending the writings of Lao-Tzu. They attempted to expand and apply Taoist philosophy to all domains of life – the philosophy of government and leadership, the ways of everyday life and the principles of war and peace.

These wise teachers of Huainan stressed the principle of cause and effect – what gives rise to what. The issues brought up here are dealt with in Lau-Tzu's Tau-te Ching and in Sun Tzu's The Art of War, but the principle is a key principle of the Huainanzi.

Of great leaders one rarely hears.
The lesser are loved and glorified.
The worse are mocked and feared.

Lau-Tzu

Tau-te Ching

When
*society is orderly,
even a fool cannot disturb it.*

When
*society is chaotic,
even a sage cannot restore order.*

9

To blame
the Tao for being ineffective
when living in a polluted world,
is like tying down a unicorn
and expecting it to run a thousand miles.

Put a monkey in a cage
and it'll look like a pig,
not because it isn't smart and quick,
but because it has no space
to display its abilities
freely.

Even
*wise leaders must wait
for appropriate circumstances.*

Appropriate circumstances can only be found at an appropriate time and cannot be created or sought through knowledge.

The wise
leave the road and search for the Way.

Fools
cling to the Way and abandon the road.

A government's

basic task is to provide security for its subjects.
The subjects' security is based on the meeting
their needs.

The meeting of the subjects' needs
is based on not depriving them of their time.

Not depriving the subjects of their time
is based on minimizing oppression
and the government's expenditures.

Minimizing oppression and the
government's expenditures is based on
restraining desire.

Restraining desire is based on
returning to the essential nature.

Returning to the essential nature is based on
removing the burden of accretion.

Remove the burden of accretion
and you will find openness.

To be open is to be even-tempered.

Even-temperance is one of the base elements
of the Way.

Openness is the home of the Way.

Those
who can become leaders
must be able to find winners.

Those who can win over opponents
must be strong.

Those who can be strong
are capable of using the power of others.

To use the power of others
one must first win their hearts.

To win the subjects' hearts
one must have self constraint.

To have self constraint
one must be flexible.

The Tao of the

Rulership

was established because the strong
oppressed the weak,
the many offended the few,
the cunning fooled the simpleminded
and the bold attacked the timid.

Subjects kept knowledge to themselves
and did not share
the wealth they had accumulated.

This is why rulership was established,
so that all subjects would be equal and united.

When
*subjects are influenced by their leaders,
they do not follow their leaders' words;*

they follow their leaders' ways.

When
*laws are written
and a judging system is established,
yet the subjects' manners do not change,
it is because this cannot succeed
without sincerity.*

Spiritual
government is first and foremost.

Second in ranking is
to make it difficult for subject to do wrong.

Third in ranking is to reward the worthy
and punish the disruptive.

Just as

a scale is fair
insofar as it weighs accurately
and a plummet is accurate
insofar as it determines straight lines correctly,
a ruler who applies the law
without preferences and aversions
can thereby command.

Huainan Masters

Law

is what restrains and punishes.
When subjects are punished
and yet are not resentful,
this is called the Way.
When the Way is in command,
subjects have no politics.

The Tao of the

In ancient times,

those who gave fit rewards
 encouraged the subjects easily.

Those who enforced fit punishments
 prevented betrayal with minimal penalty.

Those who gave well
 were sparing with expenditures
 yet werecharitable.

Those who took well
 had high income yet were not resented.

Punishment
and penalty
are not enough
to change habits.

Only spiritual influence is significant.

Executions
and massacre
are not enough
to prevent betrayal.

Only spiritual influence is significant.

The Tao of the

*Ruling kings
do not need
to legislate
strict laws
and enforce
grave punishments.*

In ancient times,

when sage leaders ruled, laws were liberal and penalty was lenient. Prisons were empty; all subjects were reliable and acted according to the same customs. In later times the government was different. Those of high rank were avaricious without measure and those of low rank were greedy and inconsiderate. The common people were poor and miserable and they fought one another. They worked hard and accomplished nothing. Clever deceivers appeared, turning into thieves and robbers. Superiors and subordinates resented each other, orders were not executed and government officials did not strive to return to the Tao. Officials attended to trivialities while dismissing that which is essential. By reducing rewards, they increased punishments. When they tried to rule this way, disorder increased.

The Tao of the

Many

intellectuals in society have departed
from the source of the

WAY

and its power.
They claim that manners
and duties are adequate
to govern the world.
One cannot speak with them
about the art of leadership.

When

rulers are very crafty, their subjects are very devious. When rulers have many obsessions and interests, their subject are constantly pretending. When rulers are nervous, their subjects are capricious. When rulers are very demanding, their subjects are argumentative. If you do not put order into the root, but care for the branches instead, it is like arousing dust when you are trying to clean a room, or carrying a pile of inflammable materials when you are trying to extinguish a fire.

Therefore

the affairs of the sages are few and easy to handle. Their demands are simple and easy to follow. They are charitable without effort, trusted without speaking. They find without seeking. They succeed without striving. They understand reality alone, accept virtue and bestow sincerity. Everyone follows them like echoes of sound, like shadows of form. They cultivate that which is essential.

The Tao of the

When
political leaders ruin their nations
and destroy their lands,

    it is always because of their desires.

when
they are killed by others
and the whole world mocks them,

    it is always because of their desires.

Huainan Masters

In ancient days
the government demanded little
and the people had plenty.

In ancient days
Rulers were benevolent
and their ministers loyal.

In ancient days
Parents were kind
and their children obedient.

In ancient days
Everyone acted with devotion
and no one was resentful.

In ancient wars

they did not kill the young and take the old captive. But what in ancient times was considered just is now considered absurd. What in ancient times was considered honorable is now considered disgraceful. What in ancient times gave to order, now gives to chaos.

The ancient rulers

did not use the system of reward and punishment, yet people did not commit crime. But those who establish governments today are unable to give up the law to govern people. One ancient ruler restrained wild tribes just by performing a warlike dance. But those who carry out police work today cannot control the strong and violent without weapons.

*In the space of one generation
cultural and martial character
may shift significantly, insofar
as there are times at which
each is useful. In our times,
however, **military** men deny
culture and the cultivated
deny the **military**. Followers
of the **military** and followers
of culture dismiss one another
without understanding the
role that each of them play
according to their era.*

The Tao of the

Human ability

is insufficient and so cannot be solely depended upon. The demands of the Way are to be carried out in public. The laws of a malfunctioning society imply great importance to measures, and punish those who cannot attain them. They impose grave responsibility and punish those who cannot bare it. They turn difficulties into dangers and execute those who cannot deal with them.

When people are under such pressure, they become crafty so that they can fool their rulers and they become devious so that they can escape. Then, even the most strict laws and harsh punishments cannot prevent crime, because they lack sufficient power. This is why the saying goes, "When birds are at a loss they peck. When animals are at a loss they jab. And when people are at loss they begin to deceive."

People

who are enlightened can pass judgment upon rulers when they see an error, because they are not thinking about revenge. They are able to submit to the opinion of the sages when they see them, because they are not thinking about rank. They are capable of providing for the needy, because they are not thinking about their own poverty.

The Tao of the

People

in high positions are considered honorable when they are fair and not influenced by their emotions. They are therefore considered honorable yet they are not considered wise. Land owners are considered fair when they act in a standard manner without hidden devices. They are therefore considered fair, yet they are not considered wise.

When there is no official cruelty to alienate the common people and no intellectual activism to make other leaders resentful, the manners of all classes steadily continue, so the critics do not understand the state of things and cannot see what needs supervision.

This is called concealment in formlessness. Without concealment in formlessness who can master form?

Moralists

today forbid the things we desire, without investigating the essential reasons for desire.
They forbid the things that are pleasurable, without investigating the essential reasons for pleasure.
This is like trying to block a river's flow with your hands.

Moralists

cannot prevent people from desiring but they can forbid the things that are desired.
They cannnot prevent people from indulging but can forbid the things that people indulge in.
Even if fear of penalty stops people from stealing, how can that compare to breaking the people's desire to steal?

The Tao of the

A government

of ideal people
covers excellence,
destroys gaudiness,
substitutes reality
for intellectual knowledge,
emerges from the integrity
that is shared by all,
frees itself from seductive longings,
dismisses natural desire
and reduces worrying thoughts.

The reasons people commit crimes that land them in prison, or get into trouble that results in execution, is that they are barehanded and insatiable.

It is well known that evildoers cannot escape and criminals must pay the penalty. And yet the unintelligent also cannot overcome their impulses, and so they commit crimes leading to their own destruction.

The world can only be entrusted to those who are able to prevent their nation's destruction by universal aspirations and to prevent their own destruction by national aspirations.

The Tao of the

Those who
know the source of law and order,
change to adapt to their time.

Those who
do not know the source of law and order,
change with customs.

Manners and duties change with customs.

Scholars believe that they must follow
precedent, while preserving the old law
which is based on convention. They think
that otherwise they will not be able to
rule.

This is like trying to fit a square peg into
a round hole.

Rulers

*are appointed is to put an end to violence
and to suppress chaos.*

*Rulers today exploit the people's power
and turn into plunderers themselves.*

*They become like winged tigers –
why shouldn't we get rid of them?*

*If you wish to raise fish in a pond,
you must get rid of otters.*

*If you wish to raise domestic animals,
you must get rid of wolves –*

all the more so when governing people!

The Tao of the

When water is contaminated, fish suffocate.

When a government is cruel, people rebel.

Huainan Masters

When society is orderly, you protect yourself with justice.

When society is confused, you protect justice by yourself.

42

The Tao of the

Hypocrisy
cannot win a single person.

Honesty
can win a hundred men.

If rulers

look upon their subjects as upon their own children, then subjects will look upon their rulers as upon their own parents. If rulers look upon their subjects as upon their younger siblings, then subjects will look upon their rulers as upon their elder siblings. When rulers look upon their subjects as upon their own children, they will be able to dominate the world. When subjects look upon their rulers as upon their own parents, they will be able to repair the world. When rulers look upon their subjects as upon younger siblings, they will easily be willing to die for them. When subjects look upon their rulers as upon older siblings, they will easily be willing to die for them. Therefore, you cannot fight an army of parents, children and brothers, because they have already done so much for one another.

The Tao of the

Rulers

demand two things of their people: they want the people to work for their country, and they want the people to die for their country. The people hope for three things from their rulers: that the hungry be fed, that the weary be given rest and that the worthy be given reward. If the people answer the government's two demands, but the government neglects the people's their three expectations, then even if a nation is large and its people many, its army will still be weak.

The martial

ruler of Wei asked one of his ministers
what brings to the destruction of a nation.

The minister replied:

"Many victories in many wars."

The ruler then asked:

"A nation is lucky to have won many wars –
why then does this destroy it?"

The minister replied:

"When there are many wars the people become
weak. When there are many victories the government
becomes arrogant. When an arrogant government
rules a weak people, only seldom does this not bring
to the destruction of a nation."

An ancient

scholar carrying many books
met a recluse on the road.

The recluse said:

"Those who serve the public act in response to changes, and changes occur over time. Therefore, those who know the times do not act in a fixed way. Books are made of words and words come from the learned. Therefore the learned do not collect books."

When

the state of Jin marched toward the state of Chu, the noblemen of Chu asked the king to attack his enemies, but the king said:
"Jin did not attack us during the reign of our former king. If Jin is attacking us during my reign, there is no doubt that this is my fault. What can be done to make up for this disgrace?"

The noblemen said:
"Jin did not attack us during the reign of the former ministers. Now that Jin is attacking us during our own reign as ministers, this is without a doubt our fault."

The king of Chu lowered his head and cried. He then rose and bowed to his ministers. When the people of Jin heard of this they said:
"The king and his ministers are competing among themselves over who should take the blame, and so easily the king humbles himself to his subordinates. We cannot attack them."

And so, that night, Jin's army turned back and returned to its land.

This is why Lau-Tzu said:
"He who can accept the disgrace of the nation is called ruler of his land."

Once

a wise man was asked which of the six leading generals would be the first to perish. The wise man named one of them and the inquirer asked why he had chosen that general.

The wise man answered:
"In his governance strictness is considered agility, pleasure is considered enlightenment and cruelty toward subordinates is considered loyalty."

This is why Lau-Tzu said:
"When the government is unimposing the people are pure. When the government is prying, the people are flawed."

Whatever

is inappropriate in the policies of former reigns is to be abandoned, while whatever is good in the affairs of later days is to be embraced. There has never been anything fixed in manners and culture, therefore the sages established manners and culture and yet manners and culture never dominated them.

To recite

the books of the ancient kings is less effective than to hear their words. To hear their words is less effective that to grasp the significance of their words. To grasp the significance of the kings' words is something that cannot be put into words. Therefore, *"a way that can be put into words is not the eternal Way."*

When

a state replaces its leaders repeatedly and the people exploit this situation to do as they wish, and exploit this power to satisfy their desires, yet they want to adapt to the time and deal with the changes in a consistent manner and by fixed laws, it is clear that they are not capable of handling the responsibility. Therefore the manner of the sages is called the Way, and their actions are called their work. The Way, like metal and stone, does not change. Their work, like a musical instrument, needs to be tuned time and time again.

The Tao of the

*Laws
and conventions
are the tools of government,
but they are **not**
government
in themselves.*

Humanity
and justice are the base and foundation of society.

This never changes.

If people are capable of assessing their abilities and devoting time to examine their actions, then even if changes occur everyday, this is all right.

54   The Tao of the

In ancient times
people were pure,
crafts were sturdy,
commerce was simple
and women were chaste.

So government and education
were easily effective,
and manners and customs
were easily changed.

Now that society's virtues
are lessening,
and customs are weakening,
attempting to govern
a decadent people
with simple laws
is like trying to ride
a wild horse
without a bit and a bridle.

King Wen was intelligent yet wanted to learn. He therefore became wise.

King Wu was brave, yet wanted to learn. He was therefore victorious.

One who utilizes the knowledge of others becomes
wise.
One who utilizes the power of others becomes a
ruler.

The Tao of the

When

a group of people unites,
a hundred men are of surplus power.
Therefore,
if the power of one alone is trusted,
surely this will result in insecurity.

When there is
no discrimination
and each individual finds
a way of life that suits him,
then there is equality
in the world
and no one dominates another.
Sages find work for all
and so no abilities are wasted.

The Tao of the

Many people are blinded by name and reputation.

Few people see reality.

It is

the nature of the common people to be wild when young, violent when mature and greedy when old. Even one man undergoes a number of changes, so it is no wonder that leaders change their laws again and again, and countries change their leaders again and again.

If people use their positions to force their likes and dislikes upon others, then those in subordinate positions of responsibility will fear being unable to manage successfully.

The Tao of the

When

manners are created, it is enough to assist reality and clarify intentions. When music is created, it is enough to harmonize pleasure and express ideas. In a country that lacks order, words and actions negate on another. Feelings and expressions are contradictory. Manners are elaborated to the point of being tedious. Music is elaborated to the point of being licentious.

Rulinga nation is like weeding a garden.

*You need only get rid the sprouts
of the harmful weeds – that's all.*

The Tao of the

Fashions,
manners and habits are not in people's nature,
but in what people absorb from the outside.

Human nature is innocent.

But when immersed in manners for long, it changes.
When people's natures change,
they forget the origin
and adapt to a seeming nature.

Those who

*have found the Way,
change from without
but not from within.
Their outward changes
allow them to enter human society.
The fact that
they do not change inwardly
allows them to remain whole.
Therefore they have
a stable inner life,
while outwardly
they are able to adjust
to the changes in others.*

The Tao of the

Those who

are afraid of touching fire, though they have never been burned, see the possibility of being burned. Those who are afraid of holding a sword, though they have never been injured, see the possibility of being injured. Therefore, those with strong perception are capable of understanding what has not yet occurred, and by observing a single organ, are able to perceive the whole body.

Treacherous

ministers confuse their ignorant leaders and narrow-minded people are suspicious of the cultivated. This can be seen even when subtle and clearly recognized only by sages.

Those who

ruled in ancient times surely understood the true conditions of human nature and destiny. Their actions may not have been the same, but in their actions they all followed the Tao.

In ancient times
vehicles were not painted or engraved.
Artists did not engage in two crafts.
Scholars did not attain two positions simultaneously.

Each engaged in their own work,
without interfering with one another.
People found what suited them.
All was at ease.

The Tao of the

Asking
for fire
is not as good as
attaining the means
to make a fire.

Depending
on someone
to fetch your water
is not as good as
digging your own well.

Huainan Masters

The spirit

*passes through mountains and they cannot harm it. It
enters oceans and rivers and they cannot wet it.
It does not suffocate in a narrow place, and though
it expands through earth and heaven,
it is never filled up.*

*hose who fail to understand this may be of material
means, of artistic culture with wonderful intellectual
and literary work, but without this understanding,
none of this will help them govern the world.*

Those who

*do not see great meaning
do not know that it is not worthwhile
to live avariciously.*

Those who

*have never heard great words
do not know that it is not worthwhile
to see ruling the world
as an advantage.*

Huainan Masters

Duty
*means doing the right thing
in accordance with reason.*

Courtesy
*means controlled elegance,
exemplifying feelings.*

The Tao of the

When
vitality and spirit are weakened,

they fall to pieces.

When
the ear and the eye are unruly,

they are weakened.

Therefore,
leaders imbued with the Way
cease imagining and insisting,
and remain balanced
in a state of clarity
and openness.

Those who

gain the benefit of power
hold few assets and great responsibility.
Their possessions are little
but their domination vast.

The Tao of the

Luxurious
balconies and tall buildings are truly wonderful,
but an enlightened ruler cannot enjoy them,
if there are people in his nation
who are homeless.

Fine wine
and tender meat are truly delicious,
but an enlightened ruler cannot enjoy them
if there are people in his nation
who are hungry.

Rulers without morals take from their people without considering their strength. They collect from their subjects without assessing how much their subjects have. Men and women cannot plow and weave because they have to fulfill the demands of their rulers. Their spirit weakens and their goods are diminished.

Thus rulers and subjects
hate one another.

The Tao of the

In the master plan of nature, the result of three years cultivation produce one year of food surplus. Nine years of cultivation produce three years of surplus, eighteen years of cultivation produce six years of surplus and twenty-seven years of cultivation produce nine years of surplus. This way, even if there is a flood or a drought, people do not find themselves in great distress.

So if a country does not have food surplus for nine years, it is in shortage. If a country does not have food surplus for six years, it is in distress. If a country does not have food surplus for three years, it is poor. Therefore rulers who are human and enlightened collect little of their subjects and live moderately.

Greedy
and hardhearted rulers
oppress their subjects
and exhaust their people
to satisfy their own interminable desires.

Thus the common people cannot
enjoy the harmony of the heavens
or the benefits of the earth.

The Tao of the

Nutrition is the basis of the people.
The people are the basis of the country.
The country is the basis of the ruler.

The country is the basis of the ruler.
The people are the basis of the country.
Nutrition is the basis of the people.

The law

of ancient kings forbade hunters to diminish the herds and to take the yearlings, and forbade fishermen to empty the ponds. It forbade the setting up of traps and nets before certain times and the cutting down of the trees before their leaves had fallen. It forbade the burning of the fields before the insects went into hibernation and the killing of animals that were pregnant or nursing. It forbade the taking of eggs from nests and catching fish whose length was less than a foot.

The Tao of the

Goodwill

and justice are the means of a nation's existence. Practical virtue is the means of human life. A nation without justice will perish, even if it is vast. People without goodwill will be wounded even if they are brave.

The ruler
is the mind of the nation.
When the mind is in order
all nodes are calm.
When the mind is out of order
all nodes are distorted.

So in one whose mind is orderly,
the organs of the body forget about each other.
When a country is orderly,
the ruler and the ministers forget about each other.

The Tao of the

Humanitarianism

is the manifest of accumulated goodwill.

Social duty

*is to share human feelings and adjust
to what is appropriate for the community.*

Ancient leaders

believed that the world was light and that many things were small. They equalized death and life and adjusted to change and evolution. They embraced the mind of the great sages to mirror the feelings of all living creatures. Above, they were companions of spiritual lights. Below, they were members of creation. If those who want to learn their Way do not attain their clear illumination and profound understanding, but only preserve their laws and politics, clearly they cannot govern.

Therefore, to buy ten sharp swords, is less important than to master the art of the sword-smith.

The Tao of the

The greatest simplicity lacks form.

The most far-reaching Way lacks measure.

Therefore, the heavens are round though they have no set boundaries, and the earth is straight though it was not set to a ruler.

Huainan Masters

Those who

value life do not destroy themselves for material gain. Those who follow ethics do not spare themselves when they find difficulty. Those greedy for money neglect their health when they spot a chance to make a profit. Those who want a good name do not try to attain it unjustly.

The Tao of the

This is

the way to govern a country: The rulers need not be harsh. The officials need not be bothersome. The intellectuals need not be hypocritical. The artists need not be decadent.

Huainan Masters

In a confused society, the activists promote each other with mutual praise, while people of culture promote one another with hypocrisy.

The Tao of the

Deceptive authors
deliberately write
in a dull and confusing fashion
in order to appear clever.
Competing with sophistry
their interminable reflections
are unconvincing
and contribute nothing
to social order.

In a decadent society people use craftiness and deception to cover the things which are useless.

The Tao of the

No one has ever heard of a man who avoided breaking the law and risking penalty when he was both cold and hungry.

When
people enjoy abundance,

                                   they comply.

When
people suffer shortage

                                   they struggle.

When
people comply

                  it results in justice and kindness.

When
people struggle

                    it results in violence and chaos.

The Tao of the

Kindling

is not sold in the forest and fish are not sold by the pond, for there is abundance in these places. So when there is abundance, desires reduce.

When desires are minimal,
quarrels come to an end.

When
*society is orderly, the common people are
honest and cannot be seduced by profit.*

When
*society is disorderly,
the elite are corrupted
and cannot be stopped by the law.*

The Tao of the

The behavior

of the sage kings never offended the people and so even when the kings were at ease everyone was silent.

The evil kings denied the truth bearers and treated them like criminals and so when the kings were at ease everything was destroyed.

When likes and dislikes began to have their say, order and chaos disappeared.

In ancient times

there were people who lived in the primeval unknown
and their spirits and talents were not manifested.
Nothing upset them so they were happy and quiet.
Harmful energies diffused and did not hurt them.
In those days people were wild. They couldn't tell
east from west. They wandered around gathering
food and then drummed their bellies and danced
while they ate. Their relationships were based on
natural harmony and they ate the fruit of the land.
Culture is a method of uniting people. Feelings are
the inner connections that create an impulse to act
outwardly. If we destroy feelings with culture, we will
have no feelings. If we destroy culture with feelings,
we will have no culture.
When culture is in order and feelings are being
expressed, it is the peak of human development.
This means that a more complete outlook is a virtue.

Once,

rewards were not used for inducement and punishments were not used as threats. Manners, duties and conscience were not defined. There was no condemnation or praise, there was no kindness or evil. Even so, people were not aggressive, deceitful, violent or cruel toward one another. They were still unselfconscious.

When society deteriorated, there were many people and few goods. People worked hard for their living and still suffered shortage. At this point anger and contention arose, and so kindness began to be valued.

Now, that some people were kind and others evil, favoritism and partisanship developed. People became deliberately cunning and deceitful. So natural virtues were lost, and duty began to be valued.

In a government

of perfect people, mind and spirit are in place, body and nature are harmonized. In times of quiet the government absorbs virtue. In times of activity it applies reason. It acts in accordance with nature as is, and focuses on essential development. It is clear and unconstrained, so the world spontaneously adapts to it. It is calm and without desire, so people are naturally simple. There are no blessings and no disasters. There are no struggles, but the necessities of life are abundantly provided. It embraces all the land and enriches its posterity. But no one knows who or what has done it.

The Tao of the

In modern governments

high taxes are collected for hunting, fishing and trade. Hatcheries are closed, there is no place to string nets, no place to plow. The people's power is used up by corvée labor. Their wealth is exhausted by poll tax. People in their homes have nothing to eat. Travelers have no supplies. The living receive no support and the dead receive no funerals. Men sell their wives and their children to satisfy the demands of the government, and are still unable to provide what is required of them.

A society

is decadent when it stands for policies of expansion and imperialism, performs unjust military operations against innocent countries, kills innocent people and denies the heritage of the ancient sages.

Large countries attack. Small countries act defensively. The attacking army kills the people's livestock, takes he people's children captive, destroys the places that are sacred to the people and confiscates the people's prized possessions. Blood is spilled and flows to the distances, and the fields are littered with skeletons – all this to satisfy the wishes of greedy governments.

This is not what armies are for. A militia need not act in violence unless it is in order to repress violence.

The true

leaders of society make progress justly, when the time is right, and so they are not especially happy about it.

When they feel that the time is not right, they withdraw and postpone it justly, and so they are not miserable about it.

This is why an ancient baron, who gave his position up to his younger brother, and who was traditionally considered an example of virtue, died of starvation in the mountains without regretting what he had done. He gave up something that was worthless to him, and gained something that was valuable to him.

According to

the art of human leadership, matters are to be
managed without devices and taught without
words. It instructs to be pure and calm, unmoving,
consistent and uncompromising, to delegate matters
to subordinates according to procedure, so that the
duties are accomplished without strain.

When

a country has vast territory as a result of virtues and the government is honored for its virtues, this is the highest of achievements.

When

a country has vast territory as a result of justice, and the government is honored for its justice, this is second best.

When

a country has vast territories as a result of power, and the government is honored for its power, this is the lowest.

A nation that is chaotic appears full.
An orderly nation appears empty.

A nation that is on its deathbed appears lacking.
A surviving nation appears to have surplus.

Emptiness does not mean that there are no people, but that the people keep to their work.
Fullness does not mean that there are many people, but that the people engage in trivialities.

Surplus does not mean many possessions, but that desires are moderate and affairs minimal.
Lack does not mean that there are no supplies, but that the people are impulsive and their expenditures many.

The Tao of the

Greedy

and lustful people are numbed by power and profit and seduced into desiring fame and rank. They want to move up in the world through exceptional cunning, so their vitality and their spirit become exhausted daily and move further and further away.

Huainan Masters

Those who desire wealth may create disaster, while those who desire gain may do wrong.

Therefore, those who live in peace without devices will be in danger if they lose the means for their peace.

And those who govern without striving will find themselves bewildered if they lose the means with which they govern.

The Tao of the

A good rider does not forget his horse. A good archer does not forget his bow. A good ruler does not forget his people.

If rulers can truly love and benefit their people, everyone will follow them. But even a child rebels against a parent who offends him rather than loves him.

There is something of supreme importance in the world, but it is not power or status. There is great wealth in the world, but it is not gold or diamonds. There is a complete life, but it is not measured by length of years.

When you look into the source of your soul and return to its essential character, this is most important. When you are content with your feelings, this is great wealth. When you understand the difference between life and death, your life is complete.

The eyes and the ears

of the enlightened leaders are not weak. Their vitality and spirit are not exhausted. When things come up, they observe the changes, and when events occur, they respond to their developments. When there is no nearby confusion, there is a distant order.

The Tao of the

Rulers

of nations that lack law and order strive to expand their territory. They do not strive for humanity and justice. They strive to elevate their status. They do not strive for the virtue of the Way. So they neglect the means of survival and create means for destruction. Therefore, the ancient tyrants who were dismissed and imprisoned did not repudiate their actions and did not admit to their errors, they only regretted that they had not killed their successors when they had had the chance.

Huainan Masters

People's hearts

can be bought but cannot be taken over. People can accept the government but they will not ask for it. Trust intelligence and the people will contest it. Trust power and the people will fight it.

It is impossible to render the people completely ignorant, but it is possible to render them unable to use their intelligence against you. It is impossible to render the people completely powerless, but it is possible to render them unable to use their power against you. These two things are always important for the long run.

The Tao of the

The cunning are good at plotting.

The knowing are good at foreseeing.

Huainan Masters

The Tao

is mysterious and quiet, with no appearance or form. Its size is infinite, its depth immeasurable. Yet it takes part in human development, though it cannot be understood through ordinary knowledge.

In ancient times when Shennong, "The Agricultural Genius", ruled the earth, his spirit did not compete within his chest. He did not use his intelligence for expansion. He had a kind and truthful heart.

There were timely pleasant rain showers and the five grains flourished. There was growth in the spring, maturing in the summer, harvest in the fall and storage in the winter.

There were monthly reviews and timely considerations. At the end of the year the fruit of labor was presented and the crops of each grain was tasted in its season.

As the king, "The Agricultural Genius", treated everyone impartially the people were simple, honest and sincere. They received enough supplies without struggle. They did their work without straining their bodies. They relied on the food that heaven and earth provided and harmonized with them.

Therefore, authority was strict but never tested. Punishments were established but never put to use. Laws were simple and unelaborated.

And so the reign of Shennong was one of genius.